The BIG NEW YORK REPRODUCIBLE Activity Book!

BY CAROLE MARSH

This activity book has material which correlates with the New York State Learning Standards.

At every opportunity, we have tried to relate information to the History and Social Science, English, Science, Math, Civics, Economics, and Computer Technology New York State Learning Standards.

For additional information, go to our websites: **www.thenewyorkexperience.com** or **www.gallopade.com**.

Correlates with the New York State™
LSSS
Learning Standards for Social Studies

Published by
GALL OPADE™
INTERNATIONAL
800-536-2GET
www.gallopade.com

Reading
R **R**
Reference Research
R **R**
Reinforcement

NSSEA   **ASCD**

A Word From The Author

New York is a very special state. Almost everything about New York is interesting and fun! It has a remarkable history that helped create the great nation of America. New York enjoys an amazing geography of incredible beauty and fascination. The state's people are unique and have accomplished many great things.

This Activity Book is chockful of activities to entice you to learn more about New York. While completing mazes, dot-to-dots, word searches, coloring activities, word codes, and other fun-to-do activities, you'll learn about New York's history, geography, people, places, animals, legends, and more.

Whether you're sitting in a classroom, stuck inside on a rainy day, or—better yet—sitting in the back seat of a car touring the wonderful state of New York, my hope is that you have as much fun using this Activity Book as I did writing it.

Enjoy your New York Experience—it's the trip of a lifetime!!

Carole Marsh

The New York Experience Series

The New York Experience! Paperback Book

My First Pocket Guide to New York!

The Big New York Reproducible Activity Book

The New York Coloring Book!

My First Book About New York!

New York Jeopardy: Answers and Questions About Our State

New York "Jography!": A Fun Run Through Our State

The New York Experience! Sticker Pack

The New York Experience! Poster/Map

Discover New York CD-ROM

New York "GEO" Bingo Game

New York "HISTO" Bingo Game

Color Me!

BROWN
Like the Beaver
Brown

BLUE
Like the New York sky
Blue

YELLOW
Like New York taxicabs
Yellow

RED
Like the Big Apple
Red

NEW YORK

Black
BLACK
Like the spots on the Ladybug

Purple
PURPLE
Like the native violet

Green
GREEN
Like the leaves of the Sugar Maple

Orange
ORANGE
Like pumpkins in the fall

Our State Bird!

Connect the dots to
see New York's
beautiful state bird,
the Bluebird.

When you are done,
color the bird.

Write the bird's name
in the space below.

Bluebirds spend
spring and summer
in New York.

They have blue wings,
heads, and backs.

The breasts of
Bluebirds are white,
with an orange bib on
the top!

The Bluebird population
has grown since the 1950s.

_ _ _ _ _ _ _ _

Hats Off to West Point!

West Point is the home of the United States Military Academy (USMA) and has been important throughout America's history. General George Washington chose Thaddeus Kosciuszko to design fortifications for West Point in 1778, and Washington moved his headquarters to West Point in 1779. West Point is the oldest United States military post that has been continuously occupied.

President Thomas Jefferson established the U.S. Military Academy at West Point in 1802. Academy graduates have served in every war after the Revolutionary War! Coursework at the Academy includes military tactics, civil engineering, science, technology, and athletics. Cadets (students) earn a bachelor of science degree at graduation and become second lieutenants in the United States Army.

Answer the following questions:

1. Who designed the fortifications at West Point in 1778?

   _____

2. Which general moved his headquarters to West Point in 1779?

   _____

3. When was the U.S. Military Academy established?

   _____

4. Name two subjects cadets learn at USMA.

   _____

5. What rank are USMA graduates?

   _____

ANSWERS: 1.Thaddeus Kosciuszko 2.George Washington 3.1802 4.military tactics, civil engineering, science, technology, athletics 5.second lieutenants

Local Government

New York's state government, just like our national government, is made up of three branches. Each branch has a certain job to do. Each branch also has some power over the other branches. We call this system checks and balances. The three branches work together to make our government run smoothly.

Match each of the professionals with their branch.

This branch is made up of two houses, the Senate and the Assembly. This branch makes and repeals laws.	This branch includes the government leaders made up of the governor, as well as appointed and elected state officials. This branch makes sure that the laws are enforced.	This branch includes the court system, which consists of the local, district, and state courts. This branch interprets the laws.
A. Legislative Branch	**B. Executive Branch**	**C. Judicial Branch**

1. the governor ____

2. a local district representative ____

3. a senator ____

4. an appointed trustee of a state university ____

5. the chief justice of the State Supreme Court ____

6. the head of the Banking Department ____

7. the lieutenant governor ____

8. a city court judge ____

9. a district attorney ____

10. a member of the Assembly ____

Vote for me in 2008!

All Around New York! Bubblegram

Bubble up on your knowledge of New York's bordering states and bodies of water.

Fill in the bubblegram by using the clues below.

1. A state east of New York
2. A state northeast of New York
3. Another state east of New York and south of the answer for number one
4. A state south of New York
5. Another state south of New York
6. A Great Lake northwest of New York

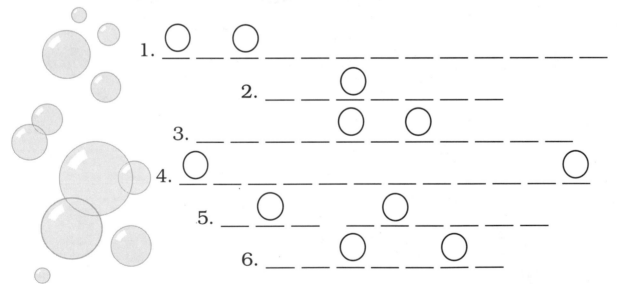

Now unscramble the "bubble" letters to discover the mystery word.
Hint: What is New York's nickname?

MYSTERY WORD: __ __ __ __ __ __   __ __ __ __ __

Borough Me In New York City!

     New York City is actually five separate communities (called boroughs) united into one enormous city. In 1898, Manhattan, which at the time was ALL of New York City, joined together with the communities of Brooklyn, Queens, the Bronx, and Staten Island. This made New York City the second-largest city in the world—only London, England was bigger!

     Each of the five boroughs has its own unique flavor and character. Manhattan is the smallest, but it is also the center of the nation's finance, culture, publishing, and fashion worlds. The Bronx, which was named for its first settler, Jonas Bronck, is the home of the world-famous Bronx Zoo and botanical gardens. Brooklyn, which sits on the southwestern tip of Long Island, has the greatest population of all the boroughs. Brooklyn also is the home of several museums, amusement parks, and other cultural sites. Queens is the home of New York's La Guardia and John F. Kennedy airports. Staten Island is the home of the famous Staten Island Ferry, and is filled with small-town neighborhoods.

Use the clues you've been given to figure out which borough is the home of these attractions!

1.   The Empire State Building: once the world's tallest building
HINT:
 + "AN"   _____

2.   Coney Island: once a premier vacation center
HINT: Another word for a stream + LYN

_____

3.   Jamaica Bay Wildlife Refuge: home to more than 300 species of birds and other small creatures
HINT:

 + S   _____

4.   Alice Austen House Museum: home of a pioneering woman photographer from 1866 to 1945
HINT: New York was the 11th _____ + 👁 + land

5.   New York Botanical Garden: 250 acres (100 hectares) of original hemlock forest
HINT: ___ ___ ___ T H E R + NX - THER

New York Wheel of Fortune, Indian Style!

The names of New York's many Native American tribes contain enough consonants to play . . . Wheel of Fortune!

See if you can figure out the Wheel of Fortune-style puzzles below! "Vanna" has given you some of the consonants in each word.

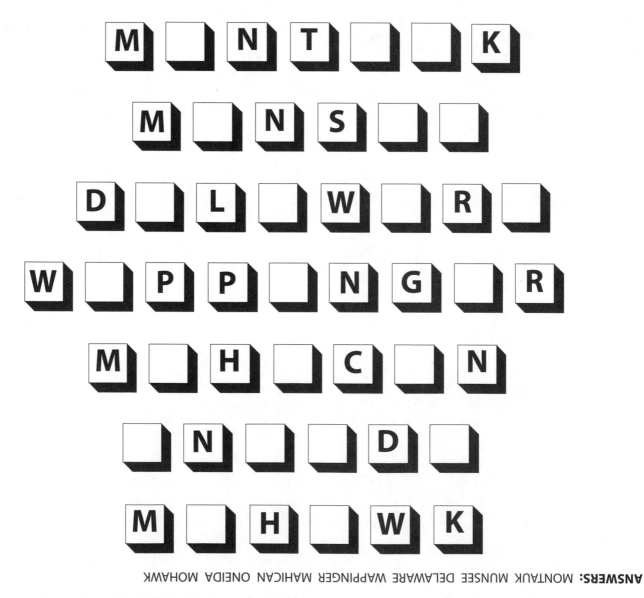

By The Skin of Our Teeth!

New York ADOPTED a state constitution in 1777, more than a DECADE before the United States had its constitution. However, New York didn't actually become a state until it RATIFIED the United States Constitution twelve years later. In 1788, New York delegates met in Poughkeepsie to vote on the U.S. Constitution. Unfortunately, two-thirds of them planned to vote "No!"

Then the delegates heard that ten other colonies had voted "Yes!" to the Constitution. New Yorkers became APPREHENSIVE that they might lose trade with the other states. After they debated BITTERLY for more than a month, New York delegates ratified the Constitution with a vote of 30 (yes) to 27 (no). New York became a state by a three-vote MARGIN!

See if you can figure out the meanings of these words from the story above.

1. adopted:_____

2. decade:_____

3. ratified:_____

4. apprehensive:_____

5. bitterly:_____

6. margin:_____

Now check your answers in a dictionary. How close did you get to the real definitions?

In the Beginning...
there was a Colony!

In 1609, Henry Hudson sailed the *Half Moon* (a ship belonging to the Dutch East India Company) up the Hudson River as far as present-day Albany. The Dutch claimed the area and settled along the Hudson River in 1624. They named their colony New Netherland. In 1625, another group of Dutch built a town named New Amsterdam.

Help the Dutch find their way to New Netherland and New Amsterdam!

New Netherland
New Amsterdam

Finish

Start

U.S. Time Zones

Would you believe that the contiguous United States is divided into four time zones? It is! Because of the rotation of the earth, the sun appears to travel from east to west. Whenever the sun is directly overhead, we call that time noon. When it is noon in Ithaca, the sun has a long way to go before it is directly over San Francisco, California. When it is 12:00 p.m. (noon) in Corning, it is 11:00 a.m. in Chicago, Illinois. There is a one-hour time difference between each zone!

Look at the time zones on the map below, then answer the following questions:

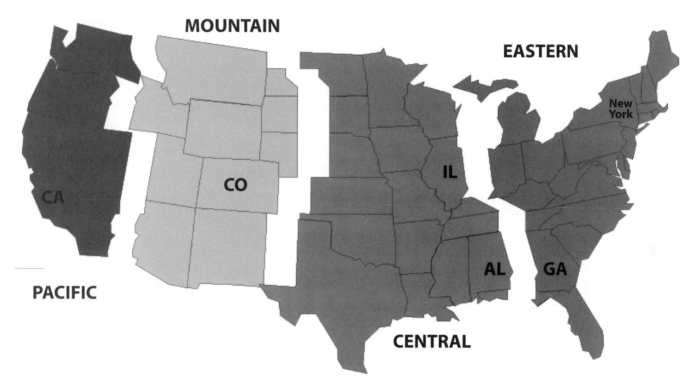

1. When it is 10:00 a.m. in Utica, New York what time is it in California? _____ a.m.

2. When it is 3:30 p.m. in Atlanta, Georgia what time is it in New York? _____ p.m.

3. In what time zone is New York located? _____

4. In what time zone is Colorado located? _____

5. If it is 10:00 p.m. in Albany, New York what time is it in Alabama? _____ p.m.

ANSWERS: 1. 7:00 a.m.   2. 3:30 p.m.   3. Eastern   4. Mountain   5. 9:00 p.m.

Sing Like a New York Bird Word Jumble!

Arrange the jumbled letters in the proper order for the names of birds found in New York.

WAXWING

OWL

FINCH

THRUSH

BLUEBIRD

ORIOLE

ROBIN

SPARROW

TITMOUSE

CROW

L W O   _ _ _

O O I R L E   _ _ _ _ _ _

N I B O R   _ _ _ _ _

R W O C   _ _ _ _

H H T U R S   _ _ _ _ _ _

S P R R W O A   _ _ _ _ _ _ _

N F I H C   _ _ _ _ _

S E U O T M I T   _ _ _ _ _ _ _ _

E L B B R U I D   _ _ _ _ _ _ _ _

N G I W X A W   _ _ _ _ _ _ _

School Rules!

The very first college in New York was King's College, which was created under a royal charter in 1754. King's College later became Columbia University, which grew in size and now also includes Barnard College. The State University of New York (SUNY) has 64 campuses and supervises all tax-supported colleges. In fact, SUNY has been in charge of New York's state colleges since 1948! SUNY's biggest campuses, complete with graduate schools, are in Albany, Binghamton, Buffalo, and Stony Brook on Long Island. By the 1990s, New York had 89 public and 221 private colleges and universities, plus 30 two-year community colleges!

Complete the names of these New York schools. Use the Word Bank to help you. Then, use the answers to solve the code at the bottom.

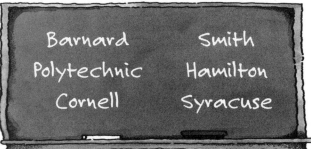

Barnard   Smith
Polytechnic   Hamilton
Cornell   Syracuse

1. __ __ __ __ __ __ _1_   College in New York City

2. __ _5_ __ __ __ __ __   University in Ithaca

3. __ __ __ _7_ __ __ __ __   University in Syracuse

4. __ __ _6_ __ _4_ __ __ __   College in Clinton

5. Rensselaer _3_ __ __ __ __ __ __ __ __ __ __ Institute in Troy

6. Hobart and William __ __ _2_ __ __ Colleges in Geneva

The coded message tells you what all college students want!

__ __ __ __ __ __ __
1   2   3   4   5   6   7

Let's Get Physical!

When we learn about New York's geography, we use special words to describe it. These words describe the things that make each part of the state interesting.

See if you can match these geographical terms with their definitions!

1. gorge
2. glacier
3. tributary
4. region
5. mound
6. waterfall
7. valley
8. strait
9. mountain range
10. canal

A. a stretch of low land lying between hills or mountains

B. a deep, narrow passage between mountains

C. a pile or heap of earth

D. a narrow body of water joining two larger ones

E. a channel dug and filled with water to allow ships to cross a stretch of land

F. a river or stream that flows into a larger body of water

G. an area of land

H. a large mass of ice that moves very slowly down a mountain or across land until it melts

I. a steep fall of a river's water from a high place

J. a group of mountains

ANSWERS: 1.B 2.H 3.F 4.G 5.C 6.I 7.A 8.D 9.J 10.E

Oh, Say Can You See . . . New York's State Flag!

New York adopted its state flag design in 1778. It shows the state coat of arms on a dark blue background. A shield is in the center of the flag, with Liberty on the left, and Justice on the right. A crown is at Liberty's feet, which symbolizes the American colonies' victory over the British in the Revolutionary War. Justice is blindfolded and holds the scales of justice. This symbolizes that all people should be treated equally under the law. The shield shows ships sailing the Hudson River with the sun rising behind them. The state motto *Excelsior*, which means "Ever Upward," is on a banner at the bottom of the shield.

Color the state flag.

Design your own Diamante on New York!

A *diamante* is a diamond-shaped poem on any subject.

You can write your very own diamante poem on New York by following the simple line by line directions below. Give it a try!

Line 1:   Write the name of an animal native to your state.

Line 2:   Write the name of your state.

Line 3:   Write the names of three of your state's important cities.

Line 4:   Write the names of four of your state's important industries or agricultural products.

Line 5:   Write the names of your state tree and state bird.

Line 6:   Write the names of two of your state's landforms.

Line 7:   Write the word that completes this sentence: New York's nickname is the _____ State.

_____

_____ _____

_____ _____ _____

_____ _____ _____ _____

_____ _____ _____

_____ _____

_____

New York, the Empire State!

Match the name of each New York state symbol on the left with its picture.

State Bird

State Flower

State Tree

State Fruit

State Animal

State Fish

Brook Trout

Rose

Apple

Beaver

Sugar Maple

Bluebird

History Mystery Tour!

New York is busting at the seams with history! Here are just a few of the many historical sites that you might visit. **Try your hand at locating them on the map! Draw the symbol for each site on the New York map below.**

Theodore Roosevelt Inaugural National Historic Site: On this site in Buffalo, Theodore Roosevelt was sworn in as president in 1901.

Fort Niagara: This fort overlooks where the Niagara River meets Lake Ontario. It was an important part of the French and Indian War, the Revolutionary War, and the War of 1812.

Phillipsburg Manor: In Sleepy Hollow, you can find Washington Irving's grave. You can also visit the home of the 18th-century Dutch trader Frederick Philipse.

National Women's Hall of Fame: Seneca Falls is called the birthplace of women's rights and is where the first women's rights convention took place in 1848. The National Women's Hall of Fame in Seneca devotes films, exhibits, and guided tours to the women's movement.

I Want to be a Part of It!

WORD BANK
Niagara
Rochester
Genesee
State
Hyde
Adirondacks
Albany
Kykuit

1. The 600-foot (183-meter) _ _ _ _ _ _ _ River Gorge is the home of three beautiful waterfalls.

2. When you visit, it might not be a good idea to go over _ _ _ _ _ _ _ Falls in a barrel!

3. The _ _ _ _ _ _ _ _ _ _ _ _ are a wonderful place to go skiing in New York!

4. The six-story mansion _ _ _ _ _ _ was the summer home built by John D. Rockefeller and his descendants.

5. At _ _ _ _ _ Line Lookout, you can see down into both Manhattan and the Hudson Valley.

6. You can see the state capitol, and maybe even poke your head in on the governor in _ _ _ _ _ _.

7. In _ _ _ _ Park, you can see three incredible homes, including the Vanderbilt Mansion.

8. You can visit Susan B. Anthony's home in _ _ _ _ _ _ _ _ _ to learn about the women's rights movement.

Soldiers at Rikers Island!

Today, Rikers and Hart Islands are part of the New York City Department of Corrections. However, during the Civil War, they served as military bases. More than 4,000 African American men formed New York's 20th, 26th, and 31st regiments of what was called the United States Colored Troops (USCT) and trained on Rikers and Hart Islands. More than 180,000 African American soldiers and sailors fought for the Union in the USCT.

Soldiers in the 20th regiment charged bravely into combat in the Battle of Port Hudson, and also fought in Texas, Florida, and Tennessee. The 26th regiment fought in South Carolina. The 31st regiment fought in Virginia and were important in the battle at Appomattox that ended the Civil War. The brave soldiers of the USCT were honored in 1998 with the unveiling of the African American Civil War Memorial in Washington, D.C.

Use information from the story above to complete the crossword.

1. Hart Island is now part of the New York City Department of _____. (ACROSS)
2. The 26th regiment of the USCT fought in South _____. (DOWN)
3. _____ and Hart Islands were military bases during the Civil War. (DOWN)
4. The 31st regiment fought in _____, at Appomattox. (DOWN)
5. The USCT fought for the _____ during the Civil War. (ACROSS)
6. The 20th, 26th, and 31st regiments of the USCT were based in _____ _____. (DOWN).

New York Rules!

Use the code to complete the sentences.

A B C D E F G H I J K L M N O P Q R S T
1 2 3 4 5 6 7 8 9 10 11 12 13 14 15 16 17 18 19 20

U V W X Y Z
21 22 23 24 25 26

1. State rules are called $\underline{\hspace{0.5cm}}$ $\underline{\hspace{0.5cm}}$ $\underline{\hspace{0.5cm}}$ $\underline{\hspace{0.5cm}}$.
   12   1   23   19

2. Laws are made in our state $\underline{\hspace{0.5cm}}$ $\underline{\hspace{0.5cm}}$ $\underline{\hspace{0.5cm}}$ $\underline{\hspace{0.5cm}}$ $\underline{\hspace{0.5cm}}$ $\underline{\hspace{0.5cm}}$ $\underline{\hspace{0.5cm}}$.
   3   1   16   9   20   15   12

3. The leader of our state is the $\underline{\hspace{0.5cm}}$ $\underline{\hspace{0.5cm}}$ $\underline{\hspace{0.5cm}}$ $\underline{\hspace{0.5cm}}$ $\underline{\hspace{0.5cm}}$ $\underline{\hspace{0.5cm}}$ $\underline{\hspace{0.5cm}}$ $\underline{\hspace{0.5cm}}$.
   7   15   22   5   18   14   15   18

4. We live in the state of $\underline{\hspace{0.5cm}}$ $\underline{\hspace{0.5cm}}$ $\underline{\hspace{0.5cm}}$ $\underline{\hspace{0.5cm}}$ $\underline{\hspace{0.5cm}}$ $\underline{\hspace{0.5cm}}$ $\underline{\hspace{0.5cm}}$.
   14   5   23   25   15   18   11

5. The capital of our state is $\underline{\hspace{0.5cm}}$ $\underline{\hspace{0.5cm}}$ $\underline{\hspace{0.5cm}}$ $\underline{\hspace{0.5cm}}$ $\underline{\hspace{0.5cm}}$ $\underline{\hspace{0.5cm}}$.
   1   12   2   1   14   25

N E W   Y O R K !

A Rough Row to Hoe!

The people who first came to New York were faced with a lot of hard work to survive in their new home. Dutch colonists first settled in the northern Hudson Valley, and then on the lower tip of Manhattan Island. Peter Minuit, governor of the New Amsterdam colony, bought the whole island from the local Native Americans for about $24!

Circle the things colonists in New York would need.

Buzzing Around New York!

Write the answers to the questions below. To get to the beehive, follow a path through the maze.

1. New York was the _____th state.
2. The first people to live in New York were the American _____.
3. The capital of New York is _____.
4. A body of water to the northwest of New York is Lake _____.
5. The _____ River is in the eastern part of the state.
6. Henry Hudson sailed the _____ _____ to the mouth of the Hudson River in 1609.
7. New York was first settled by the _____.
8. _____ _____ _____ is the largest city in New York.
9. A mountain range in southeastern New York is called the _____ Mountains.
10. Mount _____ is the highest point in New York.

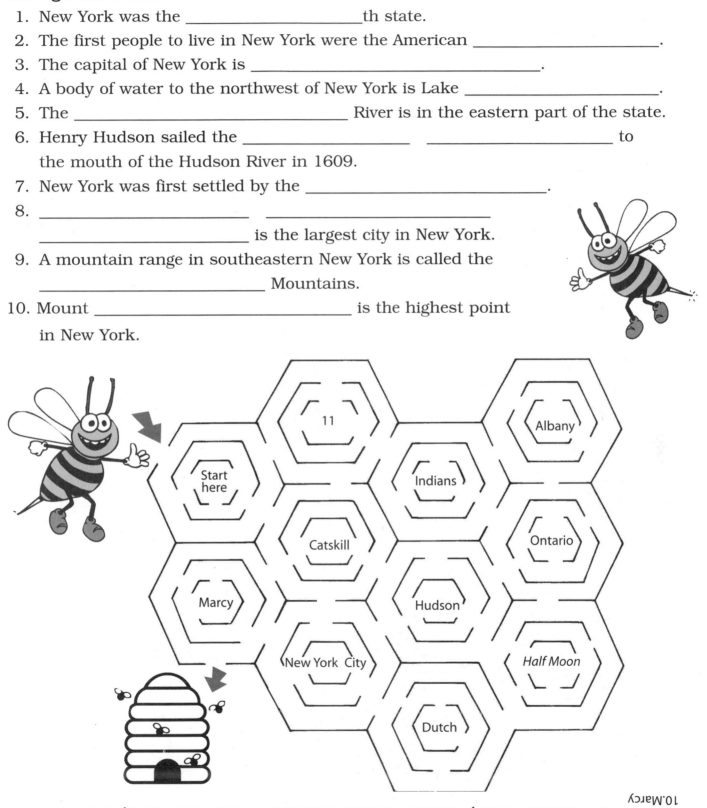

CALENDAR

New York Through the Years!

1. Giovanni Da Verrazano of
    Italy is the first European
    to enter New York's harbor.

    $6÷6=$ $3+2=$ $4-2=$ $2x2=$

2. Peter Minuit buys Manhattan
    Island for trinkets worth $24
    (according to legend).

    $5-4=$ $3x2=$ $4÷2=$ $3+3=$

3. Battle of Saratoga marks a
    turning point in the
    American Revolution.

    $6-5=$ $4+3=$ $5+2=$ $9-2=$

4. New York City becomes
    the national capital.

    $0+1=$ $6+1=$ $4x2=$ $4+1=$

5. Slavery is abolished
    in New York.

    $6-5=$ $5+3=$ $3-1=$ $8-1=$

6. Brooklyn Bridge is
    completed.

    $3÷3=$ $6+2=$ $4+4=$ $5-2=$

7. New York State Barge Canal
    is completed.

    $4-3=$ $3x3=$ $9-8=$ $2+6=$

8. State University of New York
    (SUNY) is established.

    $8-7=$ $4+5=$ $2+2=$ $8-0=$

9. Winter Olympic Games are
    held at Lake Placid.

    $4÷4=$ $6+3=$ $9-1=$ $4-4=$

10. David Dinkins is elected the
    first African-American mayor
    of New York City.

    $4-3=$ $2+7=$ $7+1=$ $3x3=$

ANSWERS: 1.1524 2.1626 3.1777 4.1785 5.1827 6.1883 7.1918 8.1948 9.1980 10.1989

Festive New York!

Every year, New Yorkers have a wide variety of festivals, fairs, and events to choose from. **See if you can match these events with the city or town in which they are held.**

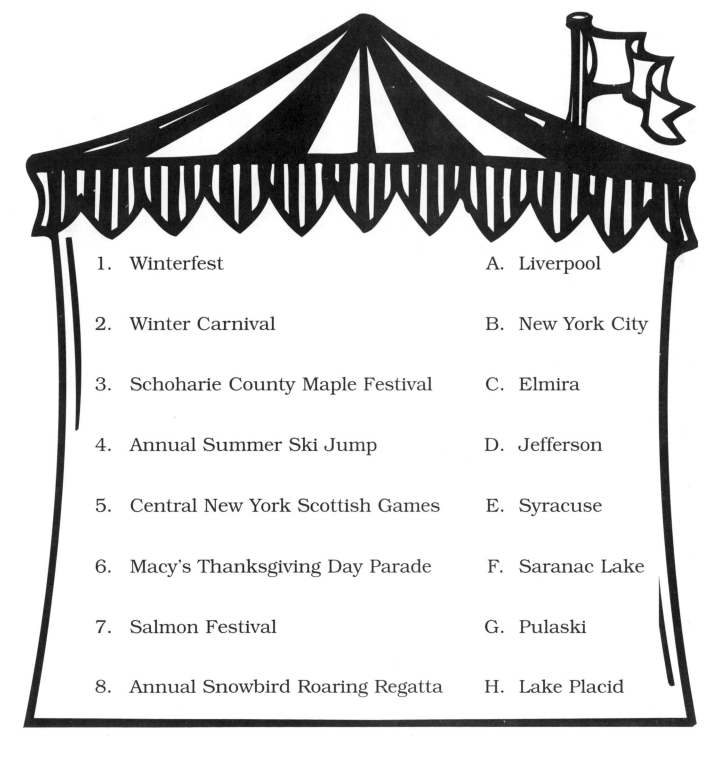

1. Winterfest   A. Liverpool

2. Winter Carnival   B. New York City

3. Schoharie County Maple Festival   C. Elmira

4. Annual Summer Ski Jump   D. Jefferson

5. Central New York Scottish Games   E. Syracuse

6. Macy's Thanksgiving Day Parade   F. Saranac Lake

7. Salmon Festival   G. Pulaski

8. Annual Snowbird Roaring Regatta   H. Lake Placid

ANSWERS: 1.E 2.F 3.D 4.H 5.A 6.B 7.G 8.C

Rhymin' Riddles

1. I am a Mid-Atlantic state, and my name starts with an "N";
   The Dutch first came, and called me "New Netherland."
   What am I?_____

   _____

2. We stretch across the land, so high and so wide;
   In northeastern New York, a beautiful sight we provide.
   What are we? _____

   _____

3. We live in Conewango, east of Chautauqua Lake;
   No electricity we use, our own furniture, bread, and cheese we make.
   Who are we?_____

   _____

4. We lived in New York before the explorers did roam;
   On the lands near rivers and mountains were our tribes' home.
   Who are we? _____

   _____

ANSWERS: 1. New York 2. Adirondack Mountains 3. Amish 4. Native Americans

New York's Venomous Snakes!

Three types of venomous (poisonous) snakes live in New York.

Using the alphabet code, see if you can find out their names.

A	B	C	D	E	F	G	H	I	J	K	L	M	N	O	P	Q	R	S	T
1	2	3	4	5	6	7	8	9	10	11	12	13	14	15	16	17	18	19	20

U	V	W	X	Y	Z
21	22	23	24	25	26

1. __ __ __ __ __ __ __ __ __ __
   13 1 19 19 1 19 1 21 7 1

2. __ __ __ __ __ __   __ __ __ __ __ __ __ __ __ __ __
   20 9 13 2 5 18   18 1 20 20 12 5 19 14 1 11 5

3. __ __ __ __ __ __ __ __ __ __
   3 15 16 16 5 18 8 5 1 4

Historical New York Women Work Wonders!

New York has been the home of many brave and influential women.
See if you can match these women with their accomplishments.
Write the letter of each lady's accomplishment next to her name.

_____ 1. Bella Savitzky Abzug

_____ 2. Frances X. Cabrini

_____ 3. Shirley Chisholm

_____ 4. Elizabeth Cady Stanton

_____ 5. Eleanor Roosevelt

_____ 6. Elizabeth Ann Seton

_____ 7. Catherine Tekakwitha

_____ 8. Sojourner Truth

A. founded the U.S. branch of the Sisters of Charity, made a saint in the Roman Catholic Church in 1975

B. author, diplomat, humanitarian, U.S. delegate to the United Nations from 1945 to 1951

C. congresswoman and leader in the women's liberation movement

D. helped to organize the Seneca Falls Convention for women's rights

E. called the "Lily of the Mohawks," first North American Indian to be a candidate for sainthood

F. social reformer and orator, born a slave

G. first U.S. citizen to be declared a saint by the Roman Catholic Church

H. first black woman U.S. representative

ANSWERS: 1.C 2.G 3.H 4.D 5.B 6.A 7.E 8.F

New York Word Wheel!

New York WORD Wheel

Independence · Tammany · Freedom · Patroons · trade · Gilded · Union · Exchange · Erie · British · Garden · Champlain

Using the Word Wheel of New York names, answer the following questions.

1. _____ were landowners who could keep a tract of land if they brought in 50 settlers within four years.
2. In 1664, New Amsterdam was invaded by the _____.
3. On July 4, 1776, delegates from New York and the other colonies signed a Declaration of _____ from England.
4. The Battle of Lake _____ was a turning point in the War of 1812.
5. The _____ Canal was built to connect the Hudson River to Lake Erie.
6. During the Civil War, New York fought on the side of the _____.
7. During the 1800s, New York City was controlled by Democrats who were members of _____ Hall.
8. Before Ellis Island, immigrants coming to New York arrived at Castle _____.
9. For the New York wealthy, the period of time that lasted from the 1890s to the 1920s was the _____ Age.
10. In 1929, the New York Stock _____ crashed on Black Tuesday.

ANSWERS: 1.Patroons 2.British 3.Independence 4.Champlain 5.Erie 6.Union 7.Tammany 8.Garden 9.Gilded 10.Exchange

Fifteen Miles on the Erie Canal!

During the 1820s, a series of canals were constructed to help connect the Hudson River to the Great Lakes. Governor DeWitt Clinton envisioned a great canal that would stretch from Buffalo on the eastern shore of Lake Erie to the Hudson River. The construction project was called "Clinton's Folly," and few people believed that a canal could be built across the 400-mile (640-kilometer) distance! In spite of the nay-sayers, the Erie Canal opened in 1825. It was the first of many such canals.

Many different kinds of boats travelled up and down the Erie Canal. Sleek packet boats carried up to 100 passengers at a time. Bullhead freighters, line boats, and scows hauled cargo, some with the help of powerful horses and mules pulling on shore! Special kinds of ships called ice breakers plowed through the frozen surface of the canal in the winter. It was certainly a different sort of traffic than what we might see today!

Below is a map of the canal system as it is in New York today. Write down which canal you would use to get from...

1. Lake Champlain to Troy: _____

2. Buffalo to Rochester: _____

3. Syracuse to Lake Ontario: _____

4. Rochester to Niagara Falls: _____

5. Plattsburgh to Albany: _____

ANSWERS: 1.Champlain 2.Erie 3.Oswego 4.Erie 5.Champlain

Mixed-Up States!

Color, cut out, and paste each of New York's five neighbors onto the map below.

Be sure and match the state shapes!

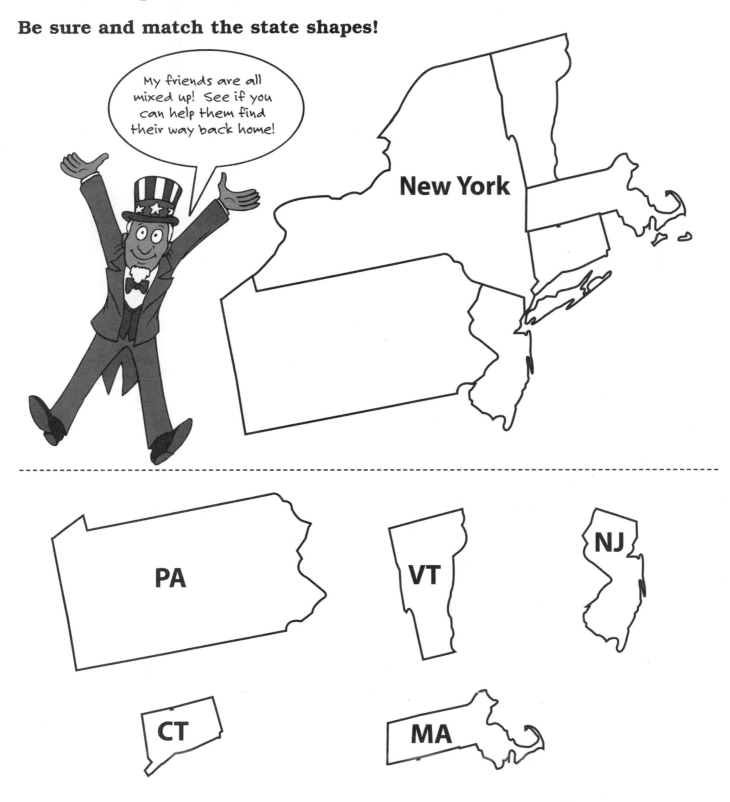

My friends are all mixed up! See if you can help them find their way back home!

New York

PA

VT

NJ

CT

MA

People and Their Jobs!

Can you identify these people and their jobs?

Put an A by the person working on a Mohawk Valley dairy farm.
Put a B by the photographer for *The New York Times*.
Put a C by the Long Island fisherman.
Put a D by the miner working in a New York limestone quarry.
Put an E by the man working in the New York pulpwood industry.
Put an F by the dancer in the New York City Ballet.

Ride the Merry Ferry!

New York City is divided into five boroughs: Manhattan, the Bronx, Queens, Brooklyn, and Staten Island. Staten Island has the smallest population of any of the New York City boroughs, and it's considerably isolated from the rest of the city. It's also just what you might think it is from its name—it's an island! Bridges connect Staten Island to New Jersey and Brooklyn, but nothing connects Staten Island to Manhattan!

People who live on Staten Island and work in Manhattan take a ferry (boat) to get from the isolated island to the busy borough. Every morning, the Staten Island ferry is filled with commuters going to work in one of the other boroughs, and every night it's full with people going home. It's one of the best bargains in the otherwise expensive New York City, and passengers have a beautiful view of the Manhattan skyline and Statue of Liberty to enjoy while they ride!

When you're on board any kind of boat, you have to use special terms to talk about directions. Label the ferry below with these terms:

bow: front of the ship
stern: back of the ship
fore: towards the bow
aft: towards the stern
port: left as you face the bow
starboard: right as you face the bow

— — — — — — — — — —

— — — —

— — — —   — — —

This arrow is pointing __ __ __ __ .

This arrow is
pointing

__ __ __ .

Politics As Usual

Our elected government officials decide how much money is going to be spent on schools, roads, public parks, and libraries. It's very important for the citizens of the state to understand what's going on in their government and how it will affect them. Below are some political words that are often used when talking about government.

Match each political word with its definition.

____ 1. Constitution

____ 2. Governor

____ 3. Chief Justice

____ 4. Assembly

____ 5. District

____ 6. Amendment

____ 7. Term

____ 8. Election

____ 9. Veto

____ 10. Bill

A. Number of years that an official is elected to serve

B. Lead Judge on the State Supreme Court

C. The chief executive

D. An addition to the Constitution

E. The selection, by vote, of a candidate for office

F. One half of New York's law-making body

G. The present version adopted in 1894, this document established New York's state laws

H. The ability to forbid a bill or law from being passed

I. Draft of a law presented for review

J. A division of a state for the purpose of electing a representative from that division

ANSWERS: 1.G 2.C 3.B 4.F 5.J 6.D 7.A 8.E 9.H 10.I

Create Your Own State Quarter!

Look at the change in your pocket. You might notice that one of the coins has changed. The United States is minting new quarters, one for each of the fifty states. Each quarter has a design on it that says something special about one particular state. The New York quarter will be in cash registers and piggy banks everywhere after it's released in 2001.

What if you had designed the New York quarter? Draw a picture of how you would like the New York quarter to look. Make sure you include things that are special about New York.

New York's Governor

The governor is the leader of the state.

Do some research to complete this biography of the governor.

Governor's name:
_____

Paste a picture of the governor here. ➤

The governor was born in this state:
_____

The governor was born on this date:
_____

Members of the governor's family:
_____
_____

Interesting facts about the governor:

_____
_____
_____
_____
_____
_____
_____
_____

The ORIGINAL Native New Yorkers!

Two major Native American language groups lived in New York around 1000 AD. The Iroquois Confederacy, which included the Oneida, Onondaga, Seneca, Mohawk and Cayuga were based in the central part of the state. The Mahican, Delaware, and Wappinger, which were Algonquian-speaking tribes, lived in southeastern New York and in the Hudson River Valley. The Iroquois and Algonquins were farmers, hunted game, and fished the many rivers and lakes of New York long before the Dutch colonists came.

Circle the things that Native Americans might have used in their everyday life.

States All Around Code-Buster!

Decipher the code and write in the names of the states that border New York.

A B C D E F G H I J K L M N O P Q R

S T U V W X Y Z

___ ___ ___ ___ ___ ___ ___ ___ ___ ___ ___ ___ ___

___ ___ ___ ___ ___ ___ ___ ___ ___

___ ___ ___ ___ ___ ___ ___ ___ ___ ___ ___ ___ ___

___ ___ ___ ___ ___ ___ ___ ___ ___ ___ ___

___ ___ ___ ___ ___ ___ ___

NEWnique New York Place Names!

Can you figure out the compound words that make up the names of these New York cities?

Centereach   _____   _____

Dayton   _____   _____

Forestport   _____   _____

Georgetown   _____   _____

Hemlock   _____   _____

Himrod   _____   _____

Inwood   _____   _____

Newark   _____   _____

Peekskill   _____   _____

Redfield   _____   _____

Redford   _____   _____

Tarrytown   _____   _____

Watertown   _____   _____

Wayland   _____   _____

Woodstock   _____   _____

Looking For a Home in the Empire State!

Draw a line from the things on the left to their homes on the right!

1. New York's governor

2. salad dressing lover

3. Army cadet

4. Washington Irving fan

5. photography historian

6. baseball enthusiast

7. hippies and artists

8. hikers and mountain bikers

9. Amish farmers

10. stockbroker

A. Sleepy Hollow

B. Woodstock

C. Catskill Mountains

D. Wall Street

E. West Point

F. Thousand Islands

G. Albany

H. National Baseball Hall of Fame

I. Conewango

J. George Eastman's house in Rochester

ANSWERS: 1.G 2.F 3.E 4.A 5.J 6.H 7.B 8.C 9.I 10.D

I Love New York, Weather or Not!

Harsh winters are a common occurrence in New York, especially in the northern part of the state. More snow falls in Buffalo, Rochester, and Syracuse than in many other American big cities. The Tug Hill Plateau near the Adirondacks gets more snow than any other place east of the Rocky Mountains! New Yorkers felt the full fury of frigid flurries falling in 1888, when an enormous blizzard dumped 40 inches (100 centimeters) of snow on the state! The coldest New York temperature was recorded in 1979, when it dropped to -52F (-47°C)! Usually, winter temperatures in January are around 21°F (-6°C).

Summers are sunny and pleasant through most of the state. Many sunbathers flock to the beaches and seashores. New Yorkers swarm to Coney Island to ride the Cyclone roller coaster, and to gobble down Nathan's Famous Hot Dogs. The highest temperature ever recorded was 108°F (42°C) in 1926, but the average July temperature is usually around 69°F (21°C).

On the thermometer gauges below, color the mercury red (°F) to show the hottest temperature ever recorded in New York. Color the mercury blue (°F) to show the coldest temperature ever recorded in New York.

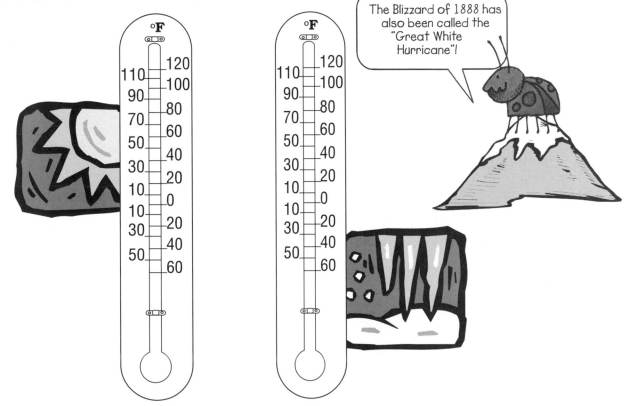

The Blizzard of 1888 has also been called the "Great White Hurricane"!

Something Fishy Here!

Thousands of years ago, glaciers covered most of New York. These huge masses of ice gouged pits into the land underneath. Those pits became the nearly 8,000 lakes that can be found throughout New York state. The largest lake that is entirely within New York's boundaries is Oneida Lake, spanning about 80 square miles (210 square kilometers) northeast of Syracuse. Also near Syracuse are the famous Finger Lakes, which are six narrow sheets of deep, blue water. In western New York is the Chautauqua Lake, where summer lectures and concerts are held at the Chautauqua Institute. Vermont shares the coast of Lake Champlain with New York.

Draw what is going on above the water line (a boat, fishermen) and add some other underwater fish friends.

The New York Scenic Route!

Imagine that you've planned an exciting exploratory expedition around New York for your classmates. You've chosen some cities and other places to take your friends.

Circle these sites and cities on the map below, then number them in the order you would visit if you were traveling north to south through the state:

_____ Finger Lakes

_____ Thousand Islands

_____ Rochester

_____ Ithaca

_____ Syracuse

_____ Binghamton

_____ Lake Ontario

_____ Long Island

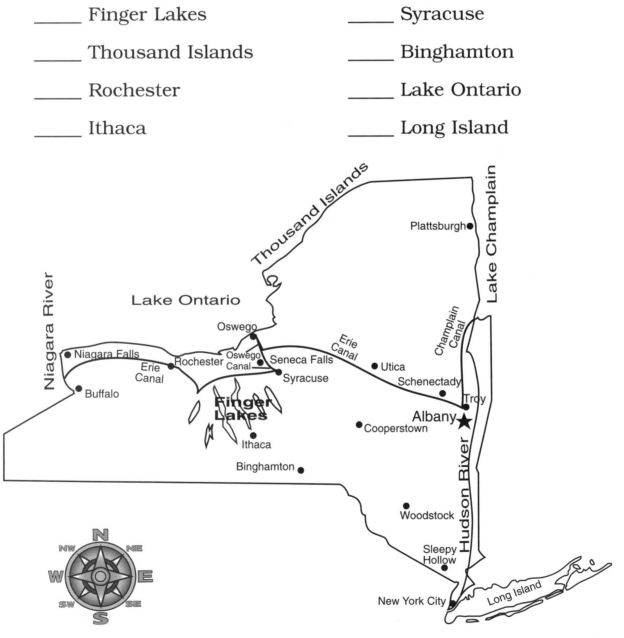

Key to a Map!

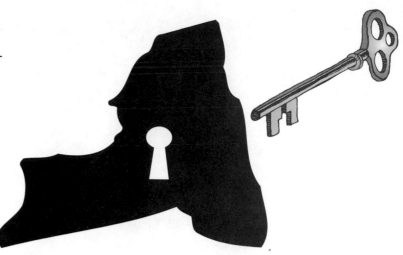

A map key, also called a map legend, shows symbols which represent different things on a map.

Match each word with a symbol for things found in the state of New York.

airport

church

mountains

railroad

river

road

school

state capital

battle site

bird sanctuary

The First Americans!

The Algonquin Indians lived in New York, which is in the Eastern Woodlands region of the United States. The types of homes they lived in were wigwams.
Color the Eastern Woodlands green.

Plains Indians lived all over the Great Plains region of North America. Some Plains Indians lived in teepees.
Color the Great Plains yellow.

Pueblo Indians lived in the Southwest region of North America. They lived in multi-story terraced buildings, called pueblos.
Color the Southwest red.

The Five Civilized Tribes and other Indians lived in the Southeast region of the United States. They lived in rectangular thatched houses called wattle and daub.
Color the Southeast blue.

Color these houses Indians lived in. Then draw a line from the type of house to the correct region.

New York Newcomers!

People have come to New York from many other states and countries. As time has gone by, New York's population has grown more diverse. This means that people of different races and from different cultures and ethnic backgrounds have moved to New York.

In the past, many immigrants came to New York from the Netherlands, England, France, Germany, and other European countries. Slaves migrated (involuntarily) from Africa. More than 12 million immigrants passed through Ellis Island between 1892 and 1954. Today, New Yorkers claim ancestors from nearly every country in the world. Only a certain number of immigrants are allowed to move to America each year. Many of these immigrants eventually become U.S. citizens.

Read the statement and decide if it's a fact or an opinion. Write your answer on the line.

1. Many of New York's early immigrants came from Europe. _____

2. Lots of immigrants speak a language other than English. _____

3. The clothing immigrants wear is very interesting. _____

4. Immigrants from England have a neat accent when they speak. _____

5. Many immigrants will become United States citizens. _____

6. People have immigrated to New York from nearly every country in the world. _____

An immigrant is a person who migrates to another country in hopes of a better life.

ANSWERS: 1.Fact 2.Fact 3.Opinion 4.Opinion 5.Fact 6.Fact

Home, Sweet Home!

Match these famous New York authors with their native or adopted hometowns. You may use some locations twice.

A = Cooperstown   B = New York City   C = Long Island
D = Morrisania   E = Manhattan   F = Rye   G = Chittenango

Match these famous New York authors with their native or adopted hometowns. You may use some locations twice.

_____ 1. Herman Melville: novelist; wrote *Moby Dick*

_____ 2 Edgar Allan Poe: author of horror stories and poems; wrote
The Pit and the Pendulum

_____ 3. Edith Wharton: Pulitzer Prize-winning author of
The Age of Innocence

_____ 4. Arthur Miller: Pulitzer Prize-winning playwright; wrote
Death of a Salesman

_____ 5. Ogden Nash: humorous and satirical poet; wrote several
collections of poems

_____ 6. Gouverneur Morris: helped to draft the U.S. Constitution

_____ 7. L. Frank Baum: author of *The Wizard of Oz*

_____ 8. Walt Whitman: author; best known for
"Oh Captain! My Captain!," a poem dedicated to the
death of Abraham Lincoln

_____ 9. James Fenimore Cooper: wrote several frontier tales, including
The Last of the Mohicans and *The Deerslayer*

_____ 10. (Marvin) Neil Simon: playwright; best known for Broadway
smashes including *Barefoot in the Park* and *The Odd Couple*

ANSWERS: 1.B 2.E 3.B 4.E 5.F 6.D 7.G 8.C 9.A 10.B

New York Spelling Bee!

Good spelling is a good habit. Study the words on the left side of the page. Then fold the page in half and "take a spelling test" on the right side. Have a buddy read the words aloud to you. When done, unfold the page and check your spelling. Keep your score. GOOD LUCK.

Adirondack _____

agriculture _____

Amsterdam _____

borough _____

Buffalo _____

economy _____

garment _____

government _____

immigrant _____

Iroquois _____

Kennedy _____

legislature _____

Manhattan _____

manufacturing _____

Niagara _____

Staten _____

transportation _____

Each word is worth 5 points. 85 is a perfect score. How many did you get right?

Suffering Until Suffrage in New York!

Before the 19th Amendment to the United States Constitution, women were unable to vote in the United States. In 1848, Elizabeth Cady Stanton, Lucretia Coffin Mott, and many other women attended the first women's rights convention in Seneca Falls. It wasn't until 1917 that women were granted suffrage in New York State. In 1920, enough states ratified the 19th amendment, and it became the law of the land. Women gained total suffrage nationally. Women today continue to be a major force in the election process.

Match the words in the left box with their definitions in the right box.

1. Amendment _____	A. The right to vote
2. Ratify _____	B. A law that is an acceptable practice throughout the nation
3. Constitution _____	C. People who could not vote in New York until 1917
4. State Senate _____	D. An addition to the U.S. Constitution
5. Law of the Land _____	E. The selection, by vote, of a candidate for office
6. Election _____	F. To give approval
7. Suffrage _____	G. The fundamental law of the United States that was framed in 1787 and put into effect in 1789
8. Women _____	H. One-half of the legislature in the state of New York

Naturally New York!

Fill in the bubblegram with some of New York's crops and natural resources. Use the letter clues to help you.

WORD BANK
VEGETABLES
WHEAT
FRUIT
LIMESTONE
CORN
OATS
OYSTERS

1. ◯ _ _ _ _ _ S

2. ◯ ◯ R _

3. ◯ _ _ _ ◯ _ _ _ _ S

4. O ◯ _ ◯

5. L ◯ _ _ _ _ ◯ _

6. _ ◯ _ _ T

7. W _ ◯ _ _

Now unscramble the "bubble" letters to find out the mystery word!
HINT: What is one way we can help to save our environment?

_ _ _ _ _ _ _ _ _ _ _ _

Can You Dig It?

New York is rich in mineral wealth. One special mineral mined there is called woolastonite which is used in matches, car bumpers, and as a tooth cleaner! Other minerals found in New York include anorthosite (which is also found on the moon!), garnet, stone, sand, limestone, zinc, talc, and salt. In fact, New York is one of the top four states in garnet, talc, and salt production!

Put the names of these minerals found in New York in alphabetical order by numbering them 1 to 10.

_____ anorthosite

_____ limestone

_____ gypsum

_____ woolastonite

_____ salt

_____ zinc

_____ gravel

_____ garnet

_____ natural gas

_____ talc

What a Brilliant Idea!

These are just some of the amazing New York inventions, inventors, and major companies.

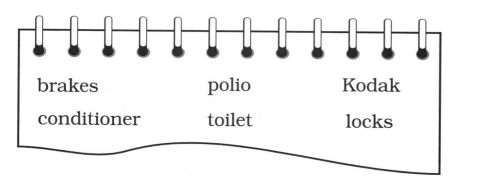

brakes   polio   Kodak

conditioner   toilet   locks

1. Jonas Salk of New York City developed the first effective __ __ __ __ __ vaccine in 1953.

2. George Eastman invented the __ __ __ __ __ camera in 1888, and developed flexible roll films.

3. Willis Carrier of Angola designed the very first air __ __ __ __ __ __ __ __ __ __ __ in 1902.

4. Thanks to George Westinghouse and his air __ __ __ __ __ __, railroad travel became much safer.

5. Linus Yale developed several types of __ __ __ __ __ which were very hard to pick.

6. Joseph C. Gayetty of New York City invented the first __ __ __ __ __ __ paper in 1857. (Thank you, Joseph!)

Famous New Yorker Scavenger Hunt!

Here is a list of some of the famous people associated with New York. **Go on a scavenger hunt to see if you can "capture" a fact about each one. Use an encyclopedia, almanac, or other resource you might need. Happy hunting!**

Humphrey Bogart _____

James Cagney _____

Bruce Cooper Clark _____

Millard Fillmore _____

Henry Louis (Lou) Gehrig _____

George Gershwin _____

Julia Ward Howe _____

Washington Irving _____

Henry James _____

John Jay _____

Jerome Kern _____

Herman Melville _____

George Mortimer Pullman _____

John D. Rockefeller _____

Anna Eleanor Roosevelt _____

Franklin D. Roosevelt _____

Theodore Roosevelt _____

Elizabeth Cady Stanton _____

Martin Van Buren _____

Walt Whitman _____

The Real Uncle Sam!

Use the words from the Word Bank to fill in the blanks in the story below. Some words may be used more than once.

Uncle Sam is a familiar _ _ _ _ _ _ of the United States government. This man with the pointy white _ _ _ _ _, red-and-white striped top hat, and blue coat can be seen on Army recruiting posters, stamps, and cartoons. What many people don't realize is that Uncle Sam isn't just a _ _ _ _ _ _; there was once a REAL Uncle Sam!

Samuel _ _ _ _ _ _ was a _ _ _ _ _ _ _ _ _ _ _ living in Troy, New York during the War of 1812. He supplied _ _ _ _ to the Army. Samuel would stamp the words U.S. _ _ _ _ on the outside of the crates he sent to the army. The local soldiers knew that Samuel was the _ _ _ _ _ _ _ _ _ _ _ who sent the _ _ _ _, and so they thought that the "U.S." on the crates stood for "Uncle Sam." It wasn't too long before people started saying "Uncle Sam" to mean "United States." James Montgomery Flagg used Uncle Sam in recruiting posters during World Wars I and II, and painted the famous _ _ _ _ _ _ to look like himself!

WORD BANK

beard	symbol
Wilson	beef
meatpacker	

Map of North America

This is a map of North America. New York is one of the 50 states.

Color the state of New York red.

Color the rest of the United States yellow. Alaska and Hawaii are part of the United States and should also be colored yellow.

Color Canada green. Color Mexico blue.

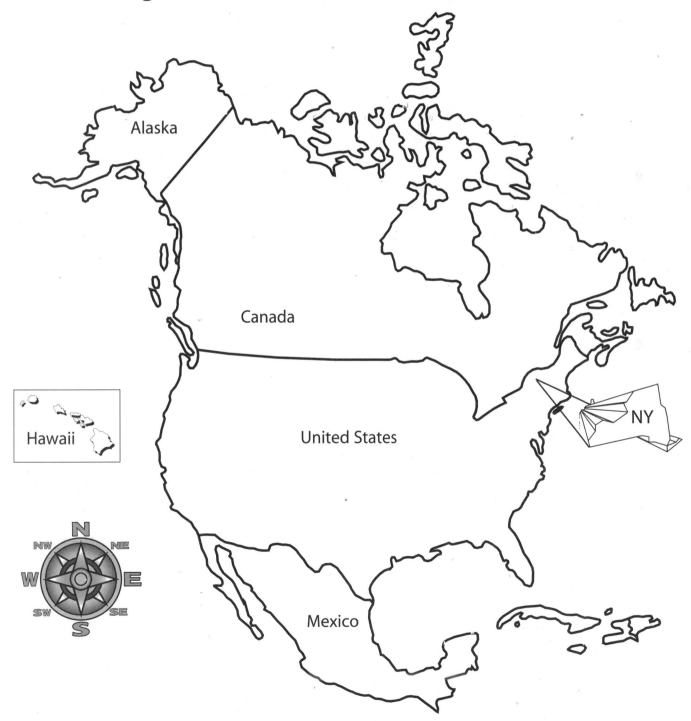

Living the Simple Life!

East of Chautauqua Lake, there is a place that seems to be frozen in time. The Conewango Amish Village is populated by a group of people called the Amish. The Amish began as a branch of the Mennonite faith. Jakob Amman, a Swiss Mennonite bishop, formed his own group in 1693, and they were named after him. Unfortunately, at that time all Mennonites were being persecuted in Europe, and the Amish were, too.

Many of the Amish fled to America to start a new life. Today, there are groups of Amish living in Pennsylvania, Canada, Ohio, New York, and Indiana. They are known for their style of dress, which is plain and simple. Women wear black dresses, bonnets, and shawls, and the men traditionally wear hats and don't trim their beards. The Amish live mostly by farming, and many of them avoid using electricity or cars.

Read the statement and decide if it's true (T) or false (F).

1. The Amish dress in bright colors. _____

2. Most of the Amish are farmers. _____

3. The Amish are named after Jakob Amman. _____

4. Most of the Amish do not use electricity or cars. _____

5. Amish men are clean-shaven. _____

6. The Amish were treated well in Europe. _____

The Empire State!

Some of these New York-related items are missing parts.
Circle the incomplete items below.

Empire State Greats!

How many of these state greats from the great state of New York do you know?

Use an encyclopedia, almanac, or other resource to match the following facts with the state great they describe. Hint: There are two facts for each state great!

1. chief U.S. negotiator at the Paris peace talks to end the Vietnam War

2. composer whose music brought together folk themes and jazz

3. professional baseball player

4. lawyer, politician, U.S. representative from 1978 to 1984

5. advisor to presidents Truman, Kennedy, and Johnson

6. lawyer and New York governor in 1875

7. playwright and politician

8. won the 1948 Academy Award for his music in the film *The Heiress*

9. first woman nominated by a major political party as its candidate for vice-president

10. held the record for career home runs until 1974

11. led the attack on the corrupt Tweed Ring in New York City

12. first U.S. woman appointed to a major diplomatic post

A. Aaron Copland

B. Geraldine Ferraro

C. William Harriman

D. Clare Booth Luce

E. Samuel Jones Tilden

F. George Herman (Babe) Ruth

ANSWERS: 1.C 2.A 3.F 4.B 5.C 6.E 7.D 8.A 9.B 10.F 11.E 12.D

New York Writers!

Fill in the missing first or last name of these famous New York writers.

1. First name: Marvin (Neil)
   Last name:_____

2. First name: _____
   Last name: O'Neill

3. First name: James
   Last name:_____

4. First name: _____
   Last name: Irving

5. First name: Henry
   Last name:_____

6. First name: _____
   Last name: Baldwin

7. First name: Eleanor
   Last name:_____

8. First name: _____
   Last name: Wolfe

9. First name: _____
   Last name: Wharton

10. First name: Lorraine
    Last name:_____

To be a reader or not to be a reader—there's only one answer!

Rip Van Winkle!

Washington Irving was an author living in Tarrytown, New York. He wrote several stories that he published in 1819 and 1820, which he based on Dutch folktales. He also wrote satires (stories that poked fun) about New York's wealthy Dutch residents. When he wrote those stories, he used the pen name Diedrich Knickerbocker. One of his most famous stories was "Rip Van Winkle."

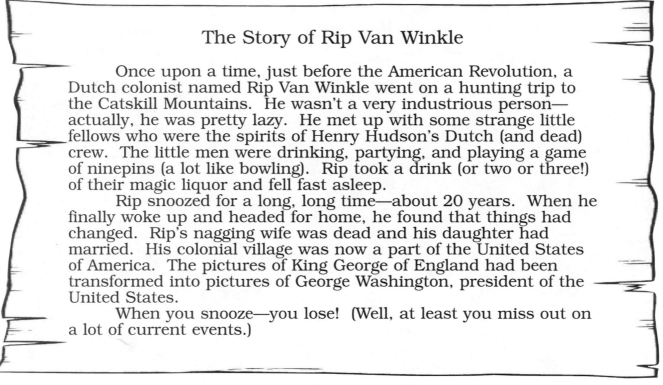

The Story of Rip Van Winkle

Once upon a time, just before the American Revolution, a Dutch colonist named Rip Van Winkle went on a hunting trip to the Catskill Mountains. He wasn't a very industrious person—actually, he was pretty lazy. He met up with some strange little fellows who were the spirits of Henry Hudson's Dutch (and dead) crew. The little men were drinking, partying, and playing a game of ninepins (a lot like bowling). Rip took a drink (or two or three!) of their magic liquor and fell fast asleep.

Rip snoozed for a long, long time—about 20 years. When he finally woke up and headed for home, he found that things had changed. Rip's nagging wife was dead and his daughter had married. His colonial village was now a part of the United States of America. The pictures of King George of England had been transformed into pictures of George Washington, president of the United States.

When you snooze—you lose! (Well, at least you miss out on a lot of current events.)

Read each statement below, and decide if it's FACT or FICTION. Write your answer on the line.

1. Rip Van Winkle drank magic liquor and fell asleep for 20 years.

   _____

2. Washington Irving wrote many stories.

   _____

3. Diedrich Knickerbocker was another name for Washington Irving.

   _____

4. Rip Van Winkle met the spirits of Henry Hudson's dead crew.

   _____

5. Ninepins is a game that is a lot like bowling.

   _____

ANSWERS: 1.fiction 2.fact 3.fact 4.fiction 5.fact

A River Runs Through It!

The state of New York is blessed with many rivers. See if you can wade right in and figure out which river name completes the sentences below!

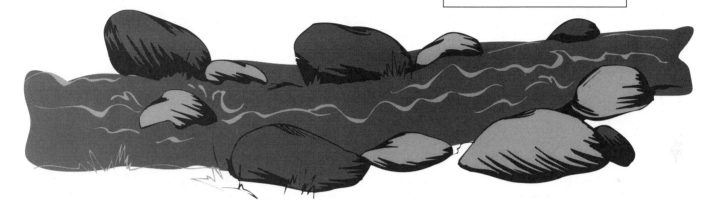

1. The _ _ _ _ _ River is not as dark as its name may imply.

2. The _ _ _ _ _ _ _ _ River flows along the border between Pennsylvania and New Jersey, and two branches are in southeastern New York.

3. I wonder if all of the fish swim upstream in the _ _ _ _ _ _ River?

4. The _ _ _ _ _ _ River is named after the man who sailed it in the 1600s.

5. You can find the _ _ _ _ _ _ _ _ _ _ _ River in both New York and Pennsylvania!

6. The name of the _ _ _ _ _ _ _ _ River sounds like something you need to play tennis.

ANSWERS: 1.Black 2.Delaware 3.Salmon 4.Hudson 5.Susquehanna 6.Raquette

Nifty New York Trivia!

But Did it Miss King Kong?
An Army Air Corps B-25 plane crashed into the Empire State Building on July 28, 1945.

Rumbles Beneath Our Feet
New York has 722 miles (1,162 kilometers) of subway track.

Call the Fashion Police!
In Carmel, it is illegal for a man to go outside while wearing a jacket and pants that don't match.

Bow-wow!
Hartsdale has a pet cemetery that was established in 1896 and contains 12,000 plots.

Mamma Mia!
Gennaro Lombardi opened the first United States pizzeria in New York City in 1895.

Wink, Wink!
According to New York state law, a person can be fined $25 for flirting!

On His Honor!
Arthur R. Eldred of Oceanside became the first Eagle Scout in 1912.

Garden Tip
On Staten Island, you may only water your lawn if you hold the hose in your hand.

Now write down another fact that you know about New York.

_____

_____

A-County-ing For Our Past!

New York has a colorful and mixed history. You can see this in many of the county names around the state. **See if you can match these names with their origins. You may need to use an encyclopedia, almanac, or other source to help you.**

COUNTY BANK

Bronx

Cattaraugus

Chautauqua

Essex

Rensselaer

Schenectady

1. Named for a county in England

   _____

2. From a Seneca Indian word meaning "bad smelling banks"

   _____

3. Named in honor of the original Dutch patroon of New Netherland

   _____

4. From a Mohawk Indian word meaning "on the other side of the pine lands"

   _____

5. Named for Joseph Bronck, the first settler north of the Harlem River _____

6. From a Seneca Indian word meaning "where the fish was taken out" _____

ANSWERS: 1.Essex 2.Cattaraugus 3.Rensselaer 4.Schenectady 5.Bronx 6.Chautauqua

Neat-o New York Gazetteer!

A gazetteer is a list of places. **Use the word bank to complete the names of some of these famous places in our state:**

WORD BANK

Crailo   Seneca
Boldt   Strong
Baseball   Sunnyside
Corning   Farmers

1. __ __ __ __ __ Castle on Heart Island

2. __ __ __ __ __ __ State Historic Site, a Dutch manor house from the 1600s

3. The National __ __ __ __ __ __ __ __ Hall of Fame in Cooperstown

4. __ __ __ __ __ __ __ __ __, the country home of Washington Irving

5. The __ __ __ __ __ __ __ Glass Works

6. The __ __ __ __ __ __-Iroquois Museum on the Allegany Indian Reservation

7. The __ __ __ __ __ __ __ Museum, with recreations of New York life from 1790 to 1860

8. The Woodbury __ __ __ __ __ __ Museum, filled with thousands of dolls

Noggin-Numbing New York Scrambles!

Unscramble the words below to get the scoop on all the state symbols of New York.

1. E R S O   _____   STATE FLOWER

2. E U L B B R I D   _____   STATE BIRD

3. N G R E T A   _____   STATE GEM

4. R B K O O   R T U O T   _____   STATE FISH

5. V B E R A E   _____   STATE ANIMAL

6. G R A S U   P L E M A   _____   STATE TREE

7. Y D L A G B U   _____   STATE INSECT

8. E A S   C R O P O N I S   _____   STATE FOSSIL

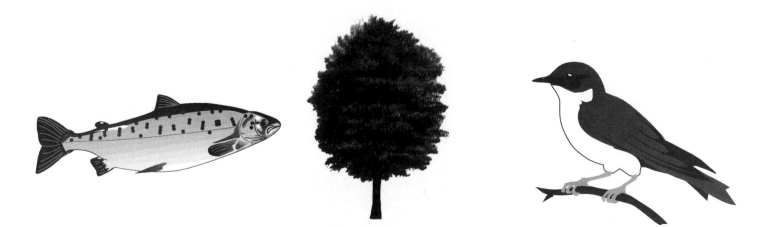

ANSWERS: 1.Rose 2.Bluebird 3.Garnet 4.Brook Trout 5.Beaver 6.Sugar Maple 7.Ladybug 8.Sea Scorpion

Industrious New York!

New York has a diverse economy that includes several industries. In fact, New York State produces more goods and services than some nations! Some industries in the state include manufacturing, farming, and tourism. New York grows a wide variety of crops. It also raises cattle, chickens, and sheep. Not only that, but New York mines produce zinc, natural gas, garnet, and many other important minerals.

Complete these sentences.

Without scientific instruments, I couldn't
_____
_____

Without natural gas, I couldn't
_____
_____

Without agriculture, I couldn't
_____
_____

Without printed materials, I couldn't
_____
_____

Without tourism, I couldn't
_____
_____

Without machinery, I couldn't
_____
_____

New York Timeline!

A timeline is a list of important events and the year that they happened. You can use a timeline to understand more about history. **Read the timeline about New York history, then see if you can answer the questions at the bottom.**

1570..........The Iroquois Federation is established.
1624..........The Dutch West India Company settles 18 families at present-day Albany.
1775..........Fort Ticonderoga is captured by Ethan Allen and Benedict Arnold.
1788..........New York becomes the 11th state.
1818..........The New York State Library is founded in Albany.
1825..........The Erie Canal is completed between Albany and Buffalo.
1886..........The Statue of Liberty is completed in New York Harbor.
1929..........Wall Street's stock market crashes, beginning the Great Depression.
1931..........The Empire State Building is completed in New York City.
1959..........The St. Lawrence Seaway opens, allowing ships to travel from New York Harbor to the Great Lakes ports.

Now put yourself back in the proper year if you were the following people.

1. If you are excited because you heard that a state library had been founded in Albany, the year is _____.

2. If you are happy because the area you live in just became the 11th state, the year is _____.

3. If you are relieved to hear that Fort Ticonderoga had been captured by the Americans, the year is _____.

4. If you are a New York stockbroker who is horrified because the market had just crashed, the year is _____.

5. If you are nervous because you were a Dutch colonist going to a new place to live, the year is _____.

6. If you are a giant gorilla that is delighted because there is a new building for you to climb, the year is _____.

7. If you are a New Yorker who is amazed at the enormous statue that has been erected in New York Harbor, the year is _____.

8. If you are a factory owner who is pleased that a new way has opened for you to ship your goods to the Great Lakes ports, the year is _____.

ANSWER: 1.1818 2.1788 3.1775 4.1929 5.1624 6.1931 7.1886 8.1959

I Am a Famous Person from New York!

From the Word Bank, find my name and fill in the blank.

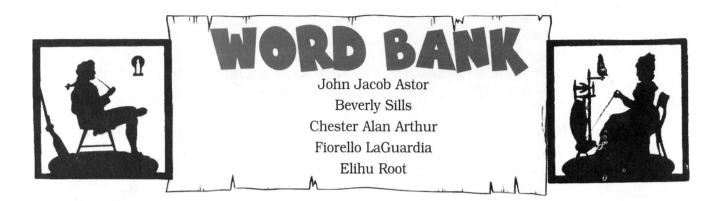

WORD BANK

John Jacob Astor
Beverly Sills
Chester Alan Arthur
Fiorello LaGuardia
Elihu Root

1. I was a lawyer and statesman born in Clinton. I helped to plan the League of Nations' World Court, and was awarded the Nobel Peace Prize in 1912.
   Who am I? _____ _____

2. I was the mayor of New York City from 1934 to 1945. I became famous for my social reform programs and my honest administration.
   Who am I? _____ _____

3. I was a fur trader and millionaire. I founded a dynasty of New York society figures and invested in Manhattan real estate.
   Who am I? _____ _____ _____

4. I was the 21st president of the United States. I became president in 1871 when James A. Garfield was assassinated.
   Who am I? _____ _____ _____

5. I was an opera soprano in the New York City Opera starting in 1955. I was also the general manager of the NYC Opera from 1980 to 1988.
   Who am I? _____ _____

New York
Native Americans!

When the colonists arrived in New York, there were two major Native American language groups (Iroquois and Algonquin) living there already. Each of these larger groups were made up of several tribes.

Draw a line from the group to its location on the map.

The Iroquoian-speaking tribes started in the central part of the state, and then took over the lands of many of the other tribes around them. The Mohawk, Oneida, Onondaga, Cayuga, and Seneca united in 1570 to create the Iroquois Confederacy (Five Nations). The Iroquois were also farmers, and lived in large bark-covered dwellings called longhouses.

Each Iroquois community was governed by a ruling council and a village chief. The whole Iroquois Confederacy was run by a common council elected by the various tribes. In fact, the Iroquois way of government was the basis for the U.S. Constitution!

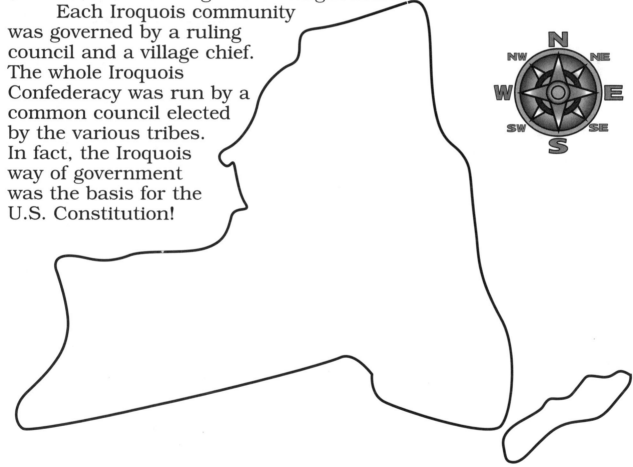

The Algonquian-speaking tribes, including the Mahican, Delaware, and Wappinger, lived in southeastern New York and up the Hudson River to Lake Champlain. The Alqonquins were primarily farmers, and raised corn, squash, and beans. They also caught fish in the Hudson River and Lake Champlain, hunted the wild game in the woods, and gathered berries, nuts, and roots.

Good Golly! New York Geography Word Search

Find the names of these New York cities in the Word Search below:

ALBANY   CORNING   HAMPTON
AUBURN   DAYTON   ITHACA
BRIGHTON   ELMIRA   MONROE
BUFFALO   FREEPORT   NEW YORK CITY
CLINTON   GRAFTON   POUGHKEEPSIE

```
P A F R E E P O R T I Y J R N
C O R N I N G E O X V H A B E
B E U M J E L M I R A A L U W
R M W G A L B A N Y R M G F Y
I T O T H U R K M X T P R F O
G T D N A K B L I E G T A A R
H M H F R L E U R P R O F L K
T D H A R O G E R B T N T O C
O L R E C D E N P N N O O W I
N L F G R A L F X S I I N N T
K H D A Y T O N T Y I X S F Y
E C D Q C L I N T O N E K S F
```

Numbering the New Yorkers!

STATE OF NEW YORK
CENSUS REPORT

Every ten years, it's time for New Yorkers to stand up and be counted. Since 1790, the United States has conducted a census, or count, of each of its citizens. **Practice filling out a pretend census form.**

Name _____ Age ☐

Place of Birth _____

Current Address _____

Does your family own or rent where you live? _____

How long have you lived in New York? _____

How many people are in your family? _____

How many females? ☐   How many males? ☐

What are their ages? _____

How many rooms are in your house? ☐

How is your home heated? _____

How many cars does your family own? ☐

How many telephones are in your home? ☐

Is your home a farm?

Sounds pretty nosy, doesn't it? But a census is very important. The information is used for all kinds of purposes, including setting budgets, zoning land, determining how many schools to build, and much more. The census helps New York leaders plan for the future needs of its citizens. Hey, that's you!!

New York Cities!

Circle Albany in red. It's the state capital.

Circle Sleepy Hollow in orange. It's where Washington Irving is buried.

Circle Cooperstown in brown. It's where the National Baseball Hall of Fame is located.

Circle Woodstock in green. An artists' colony is there.

Circle New York City in blue. It's the largest city in New York.

Add your city or town to the map if it's not here. Circle it in purple. Give it a ☺ symbol to show you live there.

Oops! The compass rose is missing its cardinal directions.

Write N, S, E, W, on the compass rose.

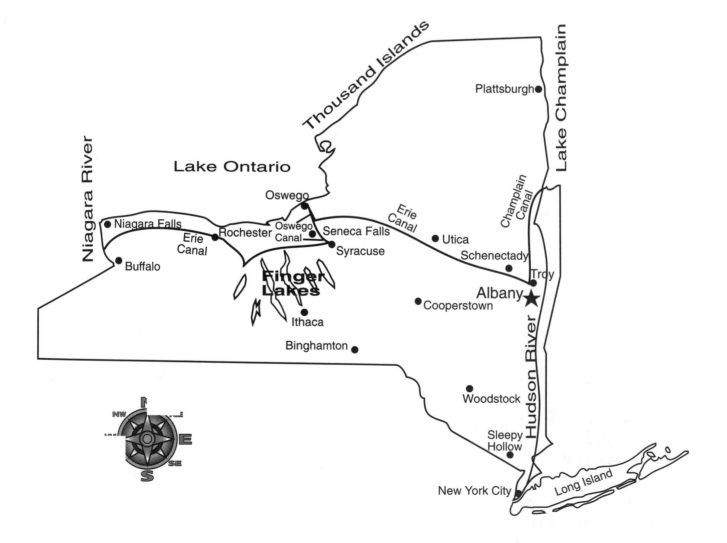

Endangered and Threatened New York!

Each state has a list of the endangered species found within their borders. An animal is labeled endangered when it is at risk of becoming extinct, or dying out completely. Land development, changes in climate and weather, and changes in the number of predators are all factors that can cause an animal to become extinct. Today many states are passing laws to help save animals on the endangered species list.

Can you help rescue these endangered and threatened animals by filling in their names below?

1. R __ __ E __ T __ T __ __ N

2. D __ A __ F W __ __ G __ M __ S __ __ L

3. G __ __ E __ S __ A T __ __ T __ E

4. B __ L __ E __ G __ __

5. P __ __ __ G __ I __ E F __ L __ __ N

6. P __ P __ __ G P __ __ V __ __

Circle the animal that is extinct (not here anymore).

I Love New York!

New York's state song is "New York, New York," written and composed by Steve Karmen.

"New York"

I love New York,
I love New York,
I love New York.
There isn't another like it
No matter where you go.
And nobody can compare it.
It's win and place and show.
New York is special.
New York is diff'rent 'cause
there's no place else on Earth
quite like New York and that's why
I love New York,
I love New York,
I love New York.

Answer the following questions:

1. How does the person singing the song feel about New York?
   _____

2. In the song, New York is win and place and...
   _____

3. Why is New York different?
   _____

4. What can nobody do to New York?
   _____

ANSWERS: (may vary slightly) 1.he/she loves New York 2.show 3.there is no other place on Earth like it 4.compare (to) it

The New York State Seal

New York's current state seal was adopted in 1882. A shield is in the center, with a blue sky and golden sun over three mountains. A river is also shown on the shield, with a ship and a sloop under sail. Above the shield, an American eagle is shown on a blue and gold wreath, and a two-thirds view of the Earth. To the right of the shield is Justice, and to the left of the shield is Liberty. The motto *Excelsior*, which means "Ever Upward," is on a silver scroll beneath the shield.

Color the state seal.

Animal Scramble!

Unscramble the names of these animals you might find in your New York backyard.

Write the answers in the word wheel around the picture of each animal.

1. *kipchnum* Hint: She can store more than a hundred seeds in her cheeks!

2. *ethiw dleait ered* Hint: He raises the underside of his tail to signal danger!

3. *nrocoac* Hint: He has very sensitive "fingers" and uses them to find food.

4. *ntseare ttoncoliat bitbra* Hint: She would love to eat the cabbages in your garden!

5. *yarg lquiersr* Hint: He scurries around all day, burying and digging up acorns!

A Quilt Of Many Counties!

New York has 62 counties. Five of the counties are the boroughs of New York City. Every city or town in New York belongs to a county.

- **Label your county. Color it red.**
- **Label the counties that touch your county. Color them blue.**
- **Now color the rest of the counties.**

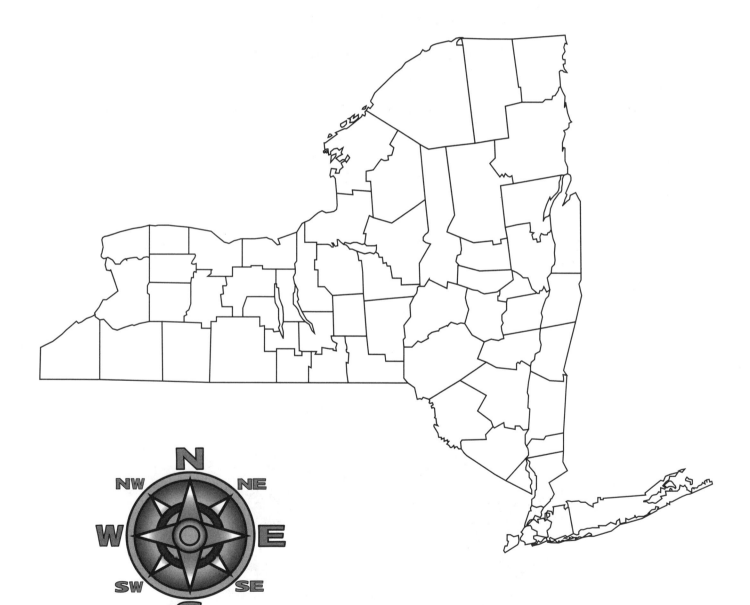

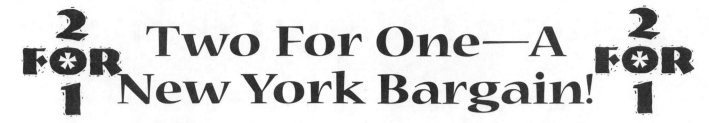

Two For One—A New York Bargain!

How many of these two-name New York places can you match? You might need a map or an atlas to help you figure them out.

1. Central	A. Upton
2. Deer	B. Miller
3. De	C. Center
4. East	D. Beach
5. Fort	E. Kalb
6. Haines	F. Forge
7. King	G. Hampton
8. Mastic	H. Baltimore
9. Mount	I. Park
10. New	J. Falls
11. Old	K. Islip
12. Reading	L. Ferry

Contributions by New York Minorities!

After World War I, thousands of African Americans moved to New York from the South. They hoped to escape racism and find better jobs. Many of them settled in Harlem, just north of Central Park in New York City. Many people of Hispanic origin also moved to New York after World War I, looking for jobs. Unfortunately, many of the newcomers could not find decent housing or employment. Between the late 1960s and the early 1970s, tensions increased and fights broke out.

However, many African Americans and Hispanic Americans have taken an active role in fixing the problems they face. Many have made and continue to make significant contributions to the state of New York and the world. Below are a few.

Try matching the people with their accomplishments.

1. Shirley Chisholm

2. Lena Horne

3. José Serrano

4. Rosa Dolores Alverio (Rita Moreno)

5. Fernando Ferrer

6. Harriet Tubman

7. Jessie Fauset

8. Carlos Manzano

A. first performer to win an Oscar, a Tony, an Emmy, and a Grammy

B. singer whose sophisticated style helped to break the stereotype of black performers

C. freed hundreds of slaves using the Underground Railroad

D. writer who participated in the Harlem Renaissance, and later taught at the Hampton Institute

E. Bronx borough president for four terms, worked to bring housing and economic opportunities to the area

F. in 1994, he became the first Colombian-born elected official in New York City history

G. first African American woman U.S. representative

H. U.S. congressman from New York

ANSWERS: 1.G 2.B 3.H 4.A 5.E 6.C 7.D 8.F

Let's Not For-get the Gar-net!

In 1969, New York chose the Garnet as its official state gem. This DAZZLING deep violet-red stone is not just another pretty face. Garnets have been PRIZED for jewelry but also have been important in industry. Its hardness helps make it useful as an ABRASIVE. It can be used in grinding wheels, saws, and high-quality sandpaper. There are actually several types of garnet, but they all share certain CHARACTERISTICS like shape. Garnet crystals are ABUNDANT and can often be found in various sizes. The state of New York is the nation's top producer of Garnets!

See if you can figure out the meanings of these words from the story above.

1. dazzling:_____

2. prized:_____

3. abrasive:_____

4. characteristics:_____

5. abundant:_____

Now check your answers in a dictionary. How close did you get to the real definitions?

Which New York Founding Person Am I?

From the Word Bank, find my name and fill in the blank.

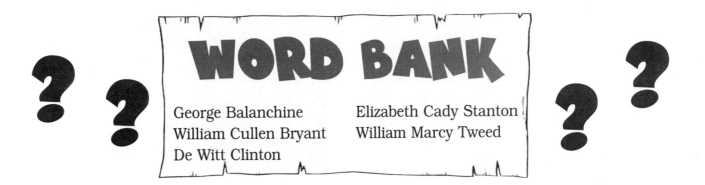

WORD BANK

George Balanchine
William Cullen Bryant
De Witt Clinton

Elizabeth Cady Stanton
William Marcy Tweed

1. I was a leader of the women's rights movement. I was an organizer of the first women's rights convention at Seneca Falls in 1848.

   WHO AM I? _____ _____ _____

2. I served in many political offices, and was governor of New York from 1817 to 1828. I also pushed for the building of the Erie Canal.

   WHO AM I? _____ _____ _____

3. I was born in Russia, and later made my home in New York City. I also founded the School of American Ballet and the New York City Ballet.

   WHO AM I? _____ _____

4. I was a political boss and founder of the Tweed Ring in the 1800s.
   I helped to swindle New York City out of millions of dollars (shame on me!).

   WHO AM I? _____ _____ _____

5. I was a poet and journalist, and editor of the *Evening Post*. I also helped to establish Central Park and the Metropolitan Museum of Art in New York City.

   WHO AM I? _____ _____ _____

ANSWERS: 1.Elizabeth Cady Stanton   2.De Witt Clinton   3.George Balanchine   4.William Marcy Tweed   5.William Cullen Bryant

It Could Happen– And It Did!

These historical events from New York's past are all out of order.

**Can you put them back together in the correct order?
(There's a great big hint at the end of each sentence.)**

- Terrorists attack the World Trade Towers on September 11. (2001)
- The British capture New York City. (1776)
- New York's first railroad, the Mohawk and Hudson, opens between Albany and Schenectady. (1831)
- The *New York Gazette*, the first newspaper in the region, is published in New York City. (1725)
- President William McKinley is assassinated at Pan-American Exposition in Buffalo. (1901)
- Chester A. Arthur becomes the 21st president. (1881)
- The Iroquois Foundation is established. (1520)
- British take over New Netherland and rename it New York. (1664)
- Giant hydroelectric power plant begins operation at Niagara Falls. (1961)
- State legislature creates an agency to guide the state education system. (1784)

1. _____

2. _____

3. _____

4. _____

5. _____

6. _____

7. _____

8. _____

9. _____

10. _____

New York Neighbors and Natives!

A state is not just towns and mountains and rivers. A state is its people! But the really important people in a state are not always famous. You may know them—they may be your mom, your dad, or your teacher. The average, everyday person is the one who helps to make the state a good state. How? By working hard, by paying taxes, by voting, and by helping New York children grow up to be good state citizens!

Match each New York person with their accomplishment.

1. Leonard Bernstein

2. Mark Wayne Clark

3. Hillary Rodham Clinton

4. Mario Matthew Cuomo

5. Geraldine Anne Ferraro

6. Horace Greeley

7. Grandma Moses

8. John D. Rockefeller

A. painter whose work was shown at New York City's Museum of Modern Art, began painting at age 76
B. newspaper editor and social reformer; founded the *New York Tribune*
C. career Army officer, U.S. commander during the Korean War
D. lawyer and politician; U.S. representative from 1978 to 1984
E. founded the Standard Oil Company in 1870; donated nearly $550 million to several organizations
F. first Italian American elected governor of New York
G. conductor, composer, pianist, and musical director of the New York Philharmonic Orchestra from 1958 to 1969
H. U.S. senator and the first First Lady to hold an elected political office

ANSWERS: 1.G 2.C 3.H 4.F 5.D 6.B 7.A 8.E

Similar State Symbols!

New York has many symbols including a state bird, tree, flag, and seal.
Circle the item in each row that is not a symbol of New York.

New York Wild Things!

The International Wildlife Conservation Park, also known as the Bronx Zoo, opened in 1899 in New York City. The zoo covers 265 acres (107 hectares) of land, and is home to about 4,000 animals. It's the country's largest urban (in a city) zoo!

The Bronx Zoo was unusual at the time of its construction because the animals were kept in natural settings surrounded by moats instead of cages. The zoo also became an important breeding center for rare animals. Visitors can be completely immersed in a jungle environment in "Jungle World," or tour the mysteries of life in Asia aboard the Bengali Express. The "World of Darkness" exhibit is also a large colony of breeding bats!

Name these animals you might find at the zoo.

New York Products Word Wheel!

Using the Word Wheel of New York product names, complete the sentences below.

1. See glassblowing and learn about glassmaking at the _____ Glass Center in the town of the same name.

2. At the George Eastman House in Rochester, you can learn about the making of _____ photography products.

3. See the fast-paced world of trading and finance at the New York _____ Exchange in New York City.

4. Go to The Original American _____ Company in Eden to learn how these funny little musical instruments are made.

5. I scream, you scream, we all scream for Perry's Ice _____ in Akron.

6. Pianists across the country can go to the _____ and Sons piano factory in Long Island City to see how their favorite instrument is made.

7. Manhattan's Lower East Side is also known as a _____ district, which was once the center of the clothing industry in New York.

8. Schenectady has been called the "City that Lights the World" because of the gigantic General _____ plants there.

9. New York City is the headquarters for many magazines, including _____.

10. In 1926, the National _____ Company (NBC) started the first commercial coast-to-coast radio station in the country.

ANSWERS: 1.Corning 2.Kodak 3.Stock 4.Kazoo 5.Cream 6.Steinway 7.garment 8.Electric 9.Newsweek 10.Broadcasting

Your Noodle Needs New York Facts!

Pop quiz! It's time to test your knowledge of New York! Try to answer all of the questions before you look at the answers.

1. New York's state bird is the...
   a. Pigeon
   b. Robin
   c. Ruffed Grouse
   d. Bluebird

2. New York became the 11th state in...
   a. 1788
   b. 1988
   c. 1688
   d. 1776

3. The current state constitution of New York was adopted in...
   a. 1621
   b. 1721
   c. 1894
   d. 1994

4. The first colony in New York was founded by the...
   a. Quakers
   b. Anglicans
   c. Dutch
   d. English

5. The capital city of New York is...
   a. New York City
   b. Albany
   c. Corning
   d. Buffalo

6. A turning point of the Revolutionary War was the Battle of...
   a. Brushy Hill
   b. Gettysburg
   c. Saratoga
   d. Ticonderoga

7. New Netherland was renamed New York by the...
   a. Dutch
   b. Germans
   c. French
   d. British

8. New York's state tree is the...
   a. Sugar Maple
   b. Hemlock
   c. Laurel
   d. Oak

9. The Erie Canal connects Lake Erie with the _____ River.
   a. Hudson
   b. Susquehanna
   c. Black
   d. Mississippi

10. Henry Hudson sailed the *Half Moon*, which belonged to the...
   a. Dutch East India Company
   b. Hudson Bay Company
   c. Land's End Company
   d. German West India Company

ANSWERS: 1.d 2.a 3.c 4.c 5.b 6.c 7.d 8.a 9.a 10.a

Papa Pulitzer!

The Pulitzer Prize is one of the most coveted awards a writer or journalist can win. Where did this prize get its beginning? A Hungarian-born journalist named Joseph Pulitzer bought the *St. Louis Post* and *St. Louis Dispatch* and merged them into the *St. Louis Post-Dispatch* in 1880. Under his guidance, the paper changed into one of the most respected newspapers in the United States.

Pulitzer moved to New York and enlarged his newspaper empire. He bought the *New York World* in 1883, then donated money to open Columbia University's School of Journalism in 1903. Wherever he went, he fought for civil reform and spoke out for clean government. He left his money to create the famous Pulitzer Prizes.

Answer the following questions:

1. Who is the Pulitzer Prize named after?

   _____

2. What papers did he buy in St. Louis?

   _____

3. What paper did he buy in New York?

   _____

4. To whom did he donate money in 1903?

   _____

5. Who can win a Pulitzer Prize?

   _____

ANSWERS: (may vary slightly) 1. Joseph Pulitzer 2. St. Louis Post and St. Louis Dispatch 3. New York World 4. Columbia University 5. writers and journalists

Hit the Heights!
See the Sights!

New York City's skyline is by far its most noticeable feature! Behemoths like the Empire State Building, the Chrysler Building, and the G.E. Building are all called "skyscrapers" because they look like they could just scrape off a bit of sky! When the Empire State Building was completed in 1931, it was the tallest building in the world, standing a majestic 1,454 feet (443 meters). The Art Deco tower of the Chrysler Building juts an incredible 1,000 feet (300 meters) into the sky! They can be quite overwhelming to see!

But, buildings aren't the only tall things in the city. The Brooklyn Bridge, which connects Manhattan Island with Brooklyn and was the first suspension bridge in the world, stands 271 feet (81.3 meters) tall. Finally, one of the most American symbols of freedom, the Statue of Liberty, stands an astounding 305 feet (91.5 meters) tall. New York sure grows 'em big!

Using the information in the paragraphs above, graph the elevations (heights) of the different things listed. The first one has been done for you.

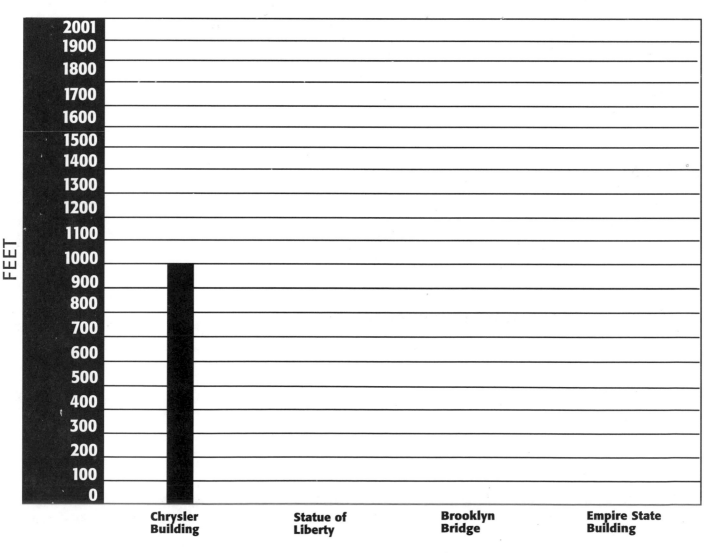

Don't Go Over in a Barrel!!

New York is blessed with one of nature's most spectacular sites—the waterfall. Niagara Falls in western New York, one of the most famous waterfalls in the world, spans the U.S.-Canadian border. On the U.S. side are the American Falls and Bridal Veil Falls. More than 500,000 gallons (2 million liters) of water fall over the cliffs every second. Other New York waterfalls include the Taughannock Falls and 18 falls that tumble through Watkins Glen State Park.

Niagara Falls was a popular stop for vacationers and honeymooners in the 19th century. Today, more than 12 million people visit these magnificent falls each year. Visitors can take an elevator from Goat Island to the foot of the falls. From there they can walk up to the crashing water.

A *haiku* is a three line poem with a certain number of syllables in each line. Look at the example below:

The first line has 5 syllables
Ni/a/gar/a Falls

The second line has 7 syllables
Splen/did wa/ter spray and flow,

The third line has 5 syllables
Wa/ter/fall di/vine!

Now, write your own *haiku* about the amazing Niagara Falls!

_____

_____

_____

Lady Liberty!

The Statue of Liberty in New York Harbor is one of the most recognizable American symbols. It was a gift from France, in honor of the friendship that grew between America and France during the Revolutionary War. The statue was built in France in 1884, moved to New York in 1885, and dedicated in 1886.

Near the statue is Ellis Island. It opened as an immigration station in 1892, and more than 12 million people passed through until it closed in 1954. Unfortunately, many of the hopeful travelers were turned back, which is why Ellis Island also became known as the Island of Tears.

The Statue of Liberty is BIG! Using these measurements, label the height, width, and length (in meters) of different parts of this picture of the Statue. (The first is done for you.)

151 feet, 1 inch (46 meters)

☞ Base to torch: 151 feet, 1 inch (46 meters)

☞ Length of right arm (holding torch): 42 feet (12.8 meters)

☞ Width of waist: 35 feet (10.7 meters)

☞ Length of tablet: 23 feet, 7 inches (7.2 meters)

☞ Width of head (ear to ear): 10 feet (3 meters)

How Big is New York?

New York is the 27th largest state in the U.S. It has an area of 53,989 square miles (139,831 square kilometers).

Can you answer the following questions?

1. How many states are there in the United States?

   _____

2. This many states are smaller than our state:

   _____

3. This many states are larger than our state:

   _____

4. One mile = 5,280 ____ ____ ____ ____

   HINT:

5. Draw a "square foot" here:

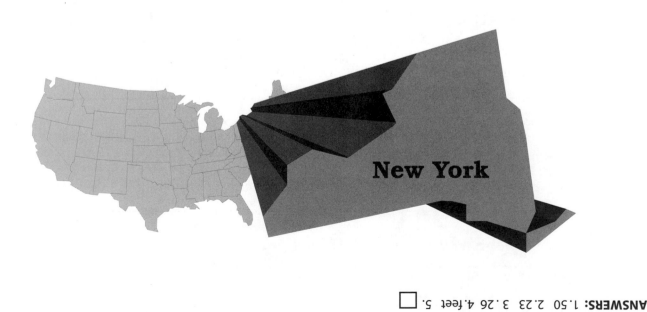

New York

Hello, Mr. President!

Did you know that several New Yorkers have been president of the United States? Martin Van Buren from Kinderhook was a lawyer who held several political offices in New York. He also was the 8th president! Millard Fillmore of Cayuga County was a state assemblyman, a U.S. congressman, and the 13th president.

Chester Alan Arthur was born in Vermont, and went to school in Schenectady. He was a lawyer, collector for the Port of New York, and the 21st president.

Grover Cleveland was born in New Jersey, but worked as a lawyer and was the mayor of Buffalo. He also was the 22nd president AND the 24th president!

Theodore Roosevelt of New York City was the commander of the Rough Riders in Cuba during the Spanish-American War, the 26th president, and the first American awarded the Nobel Peace Prize! His cousin Franklin Delano Roosevelt of Hyde Park was governor of New York, 32nd president, and planned the New Deal to help America during the Great Depression. Wow!

Which U.S. President did the following things?

1. Was the commander of the Rough Riders:
   _____   _____

2. Was the mayor of Buffalo:
   _____   _____

3. Was the collector for the Port of New York:
   _____ _____ _____

4. Planned the New Deal:
   _____ _____ _____

5. Was a state assemblyman:
   _____   _____

6. Was a lawyer from Kinderhook:
   _____ _____ _____

ANSWERS: 1.Theodore Roosevelt 2.Grover Cleveland 3.Chester Alan Arthur 4.Franklin Delano Roosevelt 5.Millard Fillmore 6.Martin Van Buren

N is for New York!

N is for New Netherland.

E is for Ellis Island.

W is for waterways and canals.

Y is for York, the Duke of.

O is for the lake named Ontario.

New York Public Library

R is for Radio City Music Hall.

K is for Kennedy International Airport.